# What is a Computer?

## Jim Drake

A computer is a machine that can do many things very
quickly. Computers need instructions called programs.
Each program makes a computer do something different.
Computer programs help us to work, have fun, learn new
things and communicate with other people. Computers
are important in many people's lives.

**Heinemann**
**LIBRARY**

First published in Great Britain by Heinemann Library,
Halley Court, Jordan Hill, Oxford OX2 8EJ
a division of Reed Educational and Professional
Publishing Ltd.
Heinemann is a registered trademark of Reed Educational
& Professional Publishing Limited.

OXFORD MELBOURNE AUCKLAND
JOHANNESBURG BLANTYRE GABORONE
IBADAN PORTSMOUTH (NH) USA CHICAGO

Designed by Visual Image, Taunton
Printed in Hong Kong

03 02 01 00 99
10 9 8 7 6 5 4 3 2 1

ISBN 0 431 04944 0

British Library Cataloguing in Publication Data

Drake, Jim
    What is a computer?. – (Log on to computers)
    1.Computers – Juvenile literature
    I.Title
    004

    ISBN 0431 04944 0

**Acknowledgements**
The Publishers would like to thank the following for
permission to reproduce photographs: BBC: O Upton p29;
Trevor Clifford: pp4, 5, 10-11, 12, 13, 14, 15, 16, 18, 20,
21, 23, 24; Format: Sally Lancaster p27; Image Bank: B
Busco p25, K Mori p22, M Tcherevkoff p17; Science
Photo Library: p6, Dr J Burgess p8, H Morgan p26, A
Syred p19; Sygma: p7, I Vimonen p28.

Cover illustration by Andy Parker.

Every effort has been made to contact copyright holders of
any material reproduced in this book. Any omissions will
be rectified in subsequent printings if notice is given to the
Publisher.

Any words appearing in the text in bold, **like this**, are
explained in the Glossary.

# CONTENTS

# WHAT COMPUTERS DO NOW

**F**ifty years ago most people had never heard of computers. This book was written on a computer. Computers helped to make the pictures. The shop where the book was bought, and the bank that the money to buy it came from, also used computers.

**There are over one hundred million computers like this in the world.**

Computers only do what they are told but they work very quickly. A **program** gives the computer instructions. Programs use special computer languages. Most computers cannot understand speech. They can take in information that is typed on a keyboard. They convert the information into a special code which sends a letter or number to the computer screen.

**Most computers cannot understand human language yet. They can understand the code on this page.**

```
                                    jindex.htm

<SCRIPT LANGUAGE = "JavaScript">
function SetCookie (name, value)
{
     var argv = SetCookie.arguments;
     var argc = SetCookie.arguments.length;
     var expires;
     var path = (argc > 3) ? argv[3] : null;
     var domain = (argc > 4) ? argv[4] : null;
     var secure = (argc > 5) ? argv[5] : false;
     var val = null;
     if (value != '') val=value;

     if (argc > 2)
          expires = argv[2]

     else
     {
          var expdate = new Date ();
          expdate.setTime (expdate.getTime () + (24 * 60 * 60 *
1000 * 365));
          expires = expdate;
     }
     //window.alert(expires+" "+path+" "+domain+" "+secure);
     document.cookie = name + "=" + escape (val) +
     ((expires == null) ? "" : ("; expires=" + expires.toGMTStri
ng())) +
     ((path == null) ? "" : ("; path=" + path)) +
     ((domain == null) ? "" : ("; domain=" + domain)) +
     ((secure == true) ? "; secure" : "");
}

function GetCookie(name) {
     var arg = name+"=";
     var alen = arg.length;
     var clen = document.cookie.length;
     var i = 0;
     while (i < clen) {
          var j = i + alen;
          if (document.cookie.substring(i, j) == arg) retu
l(j);
          i = document.cookie.indexOf(" ", i) + 1;
          if (i == 0) break;
     }
     return null;
}

function getCookieVal(offset)
{
     var endstr = document.cookie.indexOf (";", offset);
     if (endstr == -1) endstr = document.cookie.length;
     return unescape (document.cookie.substring(offset, endstr));
}

function GetCookie(name) {
     var arg = name+"=";
     var alen = arg.length;

                              Page 1
```

# COMPUTERS IN THE PAST

The first computers were made by an Englishman called Charles Babbage in 1822. They looked like complicated clocks and worked by wheels and gears. The first electronic computers were made in the 1940s. They were as big as a small house. They often broke down.

**One of Babbage's computers is in the Science Museum in London.**

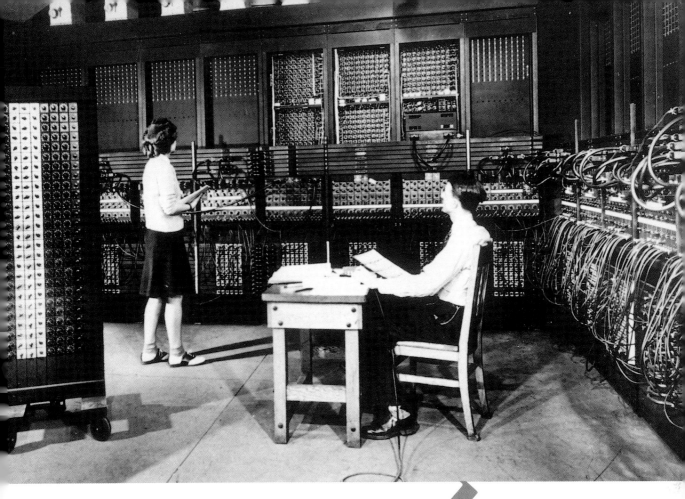

The first computers used **valves** as big as light bulbs. In the 1950s **transistors** were invented. Computers became smaller and faster. People learned how to make microchips in the 1960s and 1970s. Microchips, or '**chips**', were small enough for **personal computers** to be made. Nowadays, a computer can fit in your hand.

**This is one of the first electronic computers. A modern pocket calculator is more powerful.**

# BITS AND BYTES

**A** computer's memory is like lots of tiny electric switches. Each switch is one **bit** of information. It can be ON (1) or OFF (0). The **program** makes switches turn on or off. Eight switches (or bits) are called a byte. The pattern of ons and offs is a code that the computer understands.

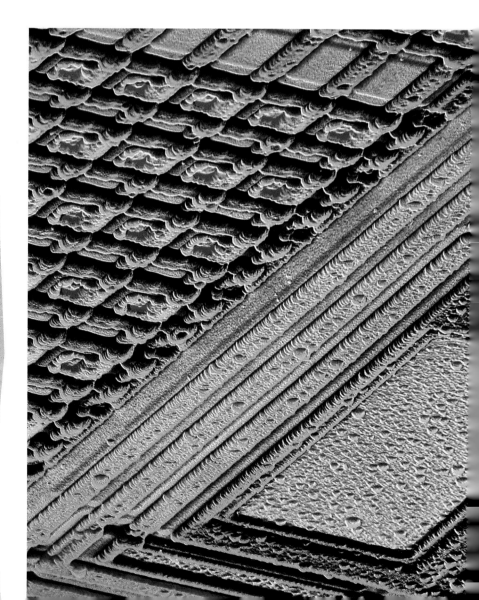

A magnified picture of a memory chip. Each of the square shapes is a tiny switch. The area shown is about as wide as two human hairs.

A computer only understands codes. Any information going into a computer is turned into codes first. In computer code, each byte means something. When you press a key, the keyboard sends a byte (the code for that key) to the computer. Sounds and pictures are also turned into codes.

9

# WHAT IS IN A COMPUTER?

**A**ll computers have these four
main parts:
- *Inputs* get codes into the system.
- *Processing* arranges codes in a
  way that the computer can
  understand.

**PROCESSING**
- **processor**
- **memory**
- **sound card**

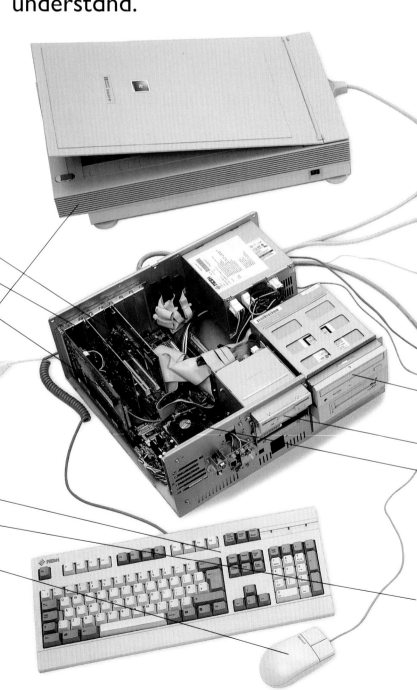

**INPUTS**
- **scanner**
- **keyboard**
- **joystick**
- **mouse**

- *Outputs* change codes into words, pictures or sounds that we can understand.
- *Storage* keeps these words, pictures or sounds so that we can use them again.

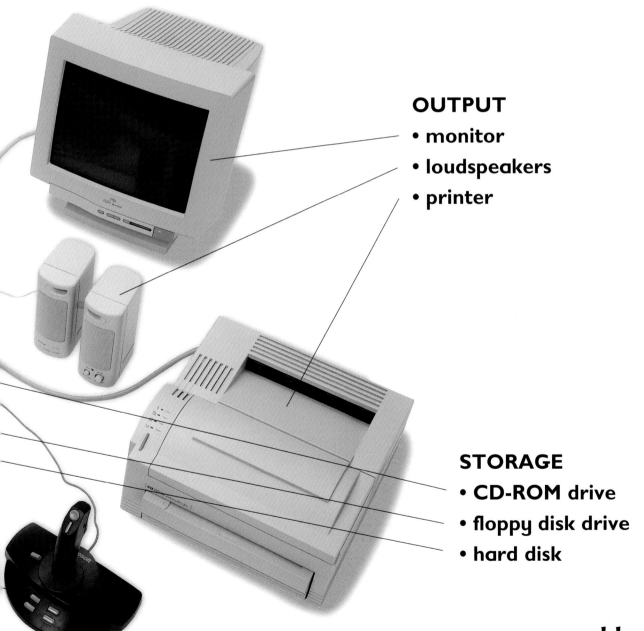

**OUTPUT**
- **monitor**
- **loudspeakers**
- **printer**

**STORAGE**
- **CD-ROM** drive
- **floppy disk drive**
- **hard disk**

# KEYBOARDS AND MICE

To tell a computer what to do we send it the right codes. A keyboard has a switch under each key. Most keyboards have over a hundred switches. When you press keys, the right codes are sent to the computer. Keyboards are used for writing text and for entering **data**.

**Pressing a key joins two metal contacts together. This tells the computer which key has been pressed.**

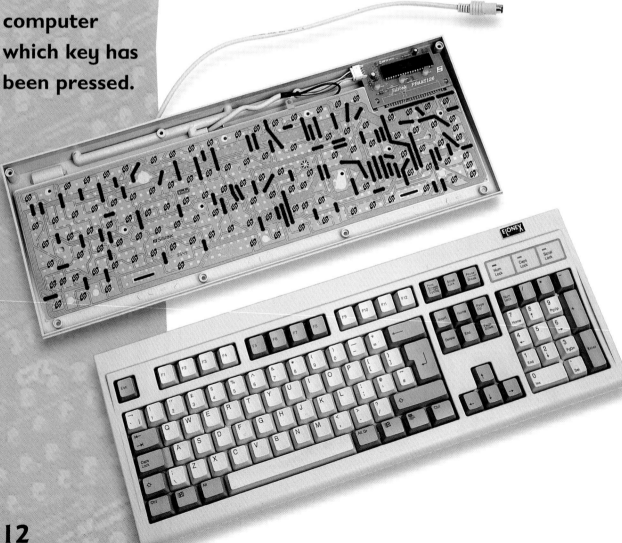

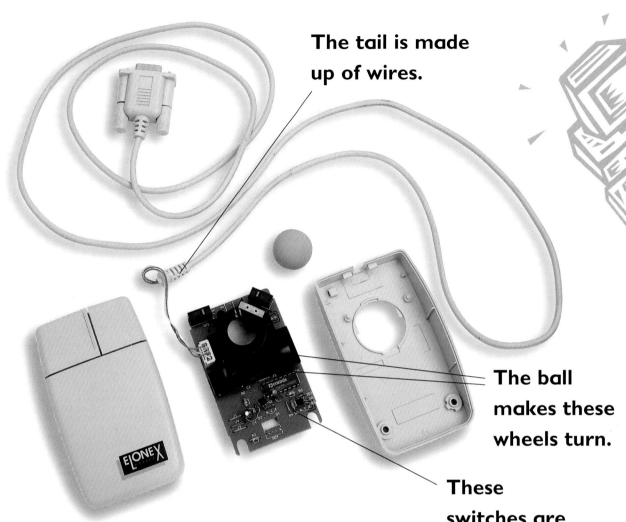

**The tail is made up of wires.**

**The ball makes these wheels turn.**

**These switches are turned on when you click a mouse button.**

A mouse is an easy way to move pointers around a screen. Mice can be used to draw shapes and pick items from a list called a menu. When the mouse moves, a ball underneath it rolls. The computer can tell how far it has moved. 'Clicking' buttons sends codes to make something happen.

# SCREENS AND PRINTERS

We cannot see computer codes. **Monitors** turn codes into patterns we can see. Everything on the screen is made of dots called pixels. Each dot can be lit up or dark. A colour screen has different coloured dots. From far away we see the picture, not the dots.

**Close up you can see the pixels that make the picture.**

14

A printer gives a picture that you can keep. It turns codes in the computer into tiny dots of ink on paper. All the words and pictures you see are made of dots joined together. Colour printers have four inks. These are mixed together to make different colours.

**Squirts of ink make dots on the paper. A full page like this has millions of dots.**

# MEMORY AND PROCESSING

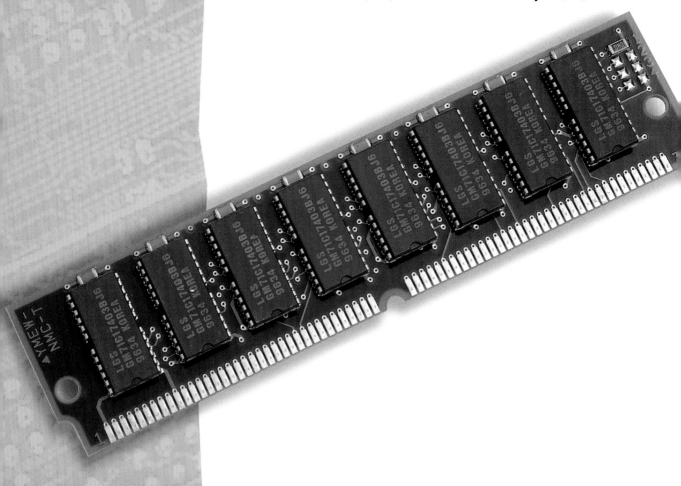

**M**emory **chips** have millions of switches to store codes. You can read the codes when you need them or write in a new code. One chip can hold over a million codes – a megabyte. This is enough to hold thousands of words. The codes disappear when the computer is turned off, unless they have been stored on disk.

A processor is the biggest chip in a computer. It does whatever a **program** tells it. It takes codes from memory and changes them. When a picture on the screen changes, the processor has to move the codes for all the pixels to a new place. A processor can change millions of codes every second.

**This microprocessor is the brains of a computer.**

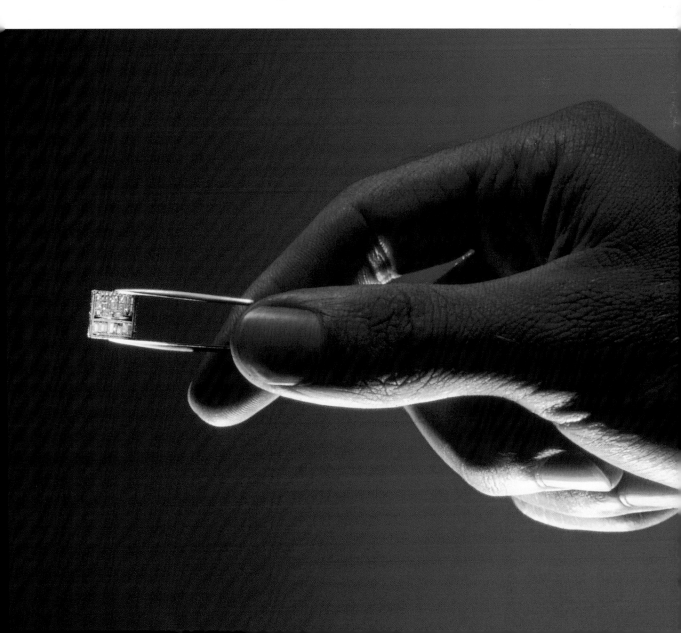

# DISKS AND CD-ROMS

**D**isks store codes when computers are turned off. They are made of thin plastic. In the plastic are millions of tiny magnets. The magnets are like the switches in the memory, but they do not need electricity. Hard disks stay in the computer. Floppy disks can be taken away from it.

**The brown plastic disk stores the codes. The case stops your fingers getting it dirty!**

**CD-ROMs** store codes too. The codes are stored as tiny pits on shiny metal. It is hard to change the codes on a CD-ROM. They are used most for information that does not need to change. A whole encyclopaedia can fit on one CD-ROM.

These marks are the pits on a CD-ROM. About 5 billion fit on one disc.

# SOFTWARE

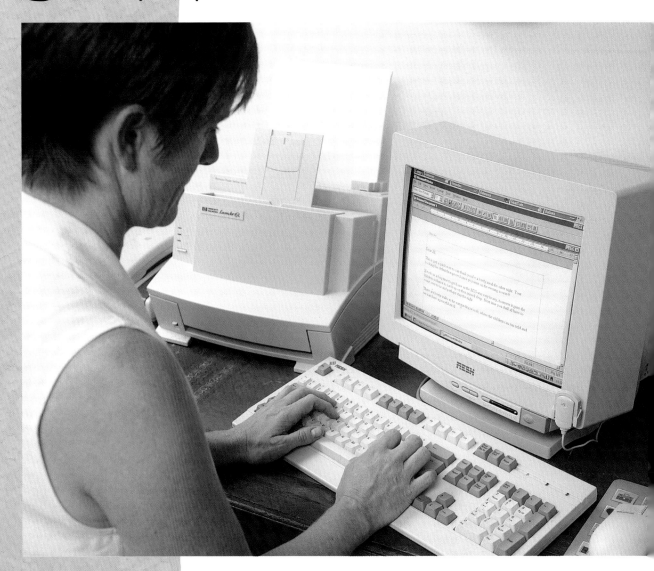

A computer cannot work at all without an operating system.

**S**oftware is another name for **programs**. All computers have an 'operating system' program. It starts when the computer is turned on. Windows™ and Mac OS™ are operating systems. All the other software on a computer is controlled by the operating system.

Word processors are software for writing. Other software helps us draw or do sums. These are called applications. Software is loaded onto a computer from disks or **CD-ROMs**. It is then kept on the hard disk. It is ready to use when you want it.

**This computer game is a type of software.**

# TALKING TO OTHER COMPUTERS

**These people can work together on their network. They can even play computer games in their breaks.**

**C**omputers can send codes to each other along wires. Several computers joined like this are called a **network**. Computers in networks can share **programs** and extra equipment like printers. Local networks can spread round a big building. You can send messages to someone on another computer in the network.

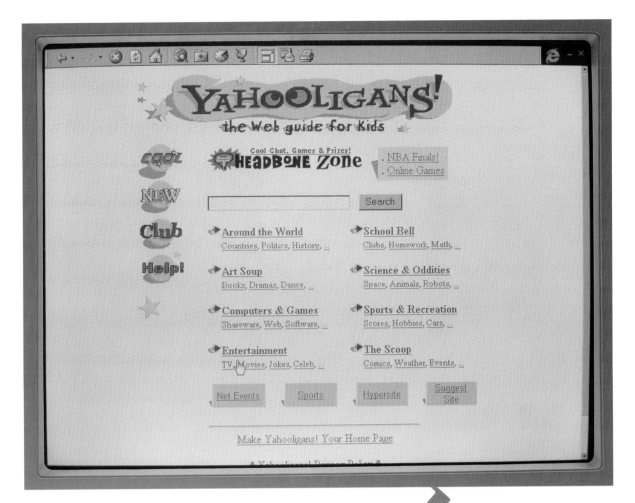

A modem turns computer codes into sounds. This lets computers send messages by telephone line. Modems also turn the sound back into codes so that another computer can read the message. Any codes can be sent. They could be writing, pictures or sound. A modem lets us send **E-mail**.

**The information on the screen has been sent from another computer.**

# PICTURES AND PIXELS

Once a scanner has changed a picture into codes, it can be changed on screen.

**A** scanner turns photos and drawings into codes. Each code stands for the colour of one pixel. Each pixel is one dot on the screen. A picture may be made of more than a million pixels. Video cards can turn TV and video pictures into computer codes.

A computer can change the codes. Special software makes this very easy to do. This will change the pictures to give 'special effects'. The colours can be changed. A picture can be stretched or squashed. Two pictures can be mixed. The pictures can be sent to other computers.

**These people may be far apart, but a computer can put their pictures together.**

# SOUND

With a microphone and **sound card**, sounds can be turned into computer codes. The sounds can then be stored in the computer's memory. The sound can be played through loudspeakers. Computers can change the codes to change the sound. Different sounds can be mixed. Special effects like echoes can be added.

Software in this computer turns the codes for speech into the codes for writing. It types on the screen whatever you say.

Some software turns your voice into codes. The computer can turn on lights or open doors when you tell it to. This helps people who cannot use their hands. Other **programs** can turn writing into speech. This can be used to help blind people read books.

**This computer turns written words into codes, then turns the codes into speech sounds. This helps blind people.**

# WHAT'S NEXT?

**C**omputers have changed more than anyone guessed. They are getting smaller, faster and smarter all the time. In your lifetime new and exciting things are sure to happen. **Virtual reality** may let us explore anywhere in the universe without leaving home.

**A computer can beat the best human chess players.**

Perhaps robots, worked by computers, will do all the things we hate – tidy up after us, for instance. Computers can already beat chess champions. One day computers might be able to think for themselves. We may not need to give them **programs** anymore.

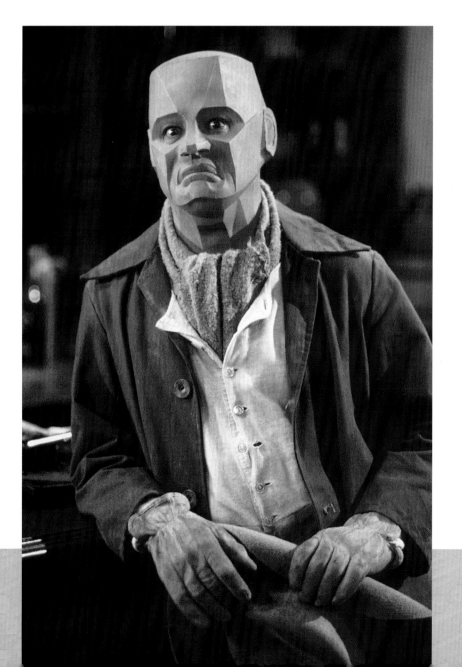

Films and television programmes often show robots that are almost like people. One day this might come true!

# GLOSSARY

**bit**   short for 'binary digit'. One switch, which is either ON or OFF, is one bit of information.

**CD-ROM**   shiny disc that can store words, pictures and music

**chip**   short for microchip, a piece of a metal called silicon containing millions of transistors

**data**   information stored on a computer

**E-mail**   messages sent between computers on a network

**module**   holds many chips and plugs into a computer. It adds space to the computer's memory.

**monitor**   a computer screen

**network**   a way of joining computers so that they can send messages to each other along wires. Computers on a network can share software.

**personal computer**  computers that are small enough to sit on a desk

**program**  the instructions that tell a computer what to do

**sound card**  lets a computer turn sounds into computer codes and back again

**transistor**  a type of electronic switch invented in 1949. Microchips can contain millions of tiny transistors.

**valves**  the first type of electronic switch. They were shaped like small light bulbs.

**virtual reality**  using computers to create illusions, so you can see things that are not really there

# INDEX